King

The SKY

Modern Publishing

A Division of Unisystems, Inc.

New York, New York 10022

CONTENTS

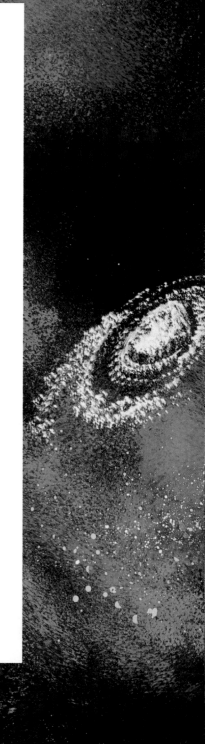

Beyond the Sky

Looking Up—What do we see when we look up? We see the clouds and the sky. Do you ever wonder what is up in the sky beyond the clouds? Way up beyond the clouds are the sun, the moon, and millions of stars. . .

The Wind

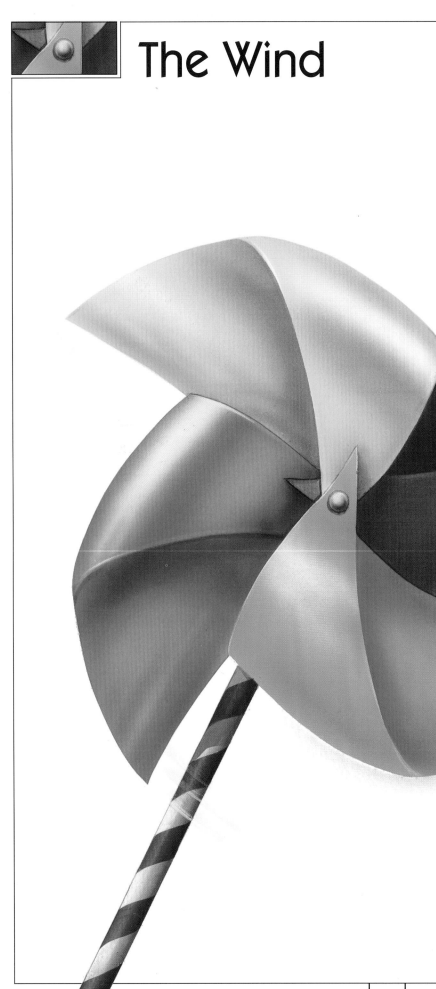

Down Here—On the ground we feel the wind blowing. It blows in our faces and makes our hats fly off. What is the wind? It is moving air. Air that is warmed by the sun rises. Cold air moves in quickly to fill its place. The moving air is the wind.

Wind from Far Away Places—The winds that blow regularly in the same direction are called "tradewinds." They are found in the warmest regions of the earth, near the equator and the tropics.

Sailboat

Monsoons—These are winds that change direction every six months. They are produced by differences between the temperatures of the continents and the oceans. The summer monsoons are hot and humid. They bring a great deal of rain to India, China, and many other countries in Asia.

Useful Wind—Before there were steamboats or motorboats people used sailboats. The wind filled the boats' sails and moved them over the water.

Wind generator

Ancient and Modern Windmills—The wind has always been very important for windmills. The wind turns their great blades, which are called "sweeps," and creates energy. A long time ago windmills were used to grind wheat into flour. Today they are used to produce "clean energy." In many parts of the world there are "wind farms" that make electricity.

Gliders—Airplanes without engines are called "gliders." They are towed up into the air by airplanes with engines. When the gliders have reached the required height, they are cut loose. Glider pilots understand wind currents and use rising warm air currents to stay up.

Windmill

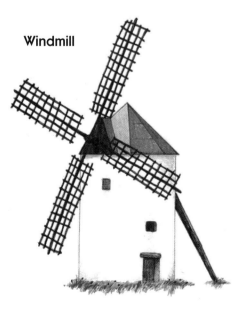

Glider

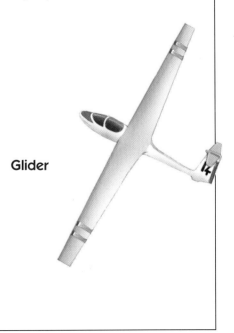

Sky Shows

cirrus   stratus

cumulus   cumulonimbus

Clouds—Warm air rises. As it rises it cools and the dampness in the air forms tiny droplets of water. These droplets turn into clouds which are carried by the wind.

All Kinds of Clouds—By watching the clouds, you may be able to tell what the weather will be like. There are many different types of clouds. The very high clouds are cirrus clouds. They tell us that the weather is changing. Below these are the stratus clouds. They are flat, gray clouds that cover the sky and bring rain. Below these are the big puffy cumulus and cumulonimbus clouds, which bring thunder storms.

Danger from the Sky—A flash of lightning is the passing of electricity between the clouds, or between the clouds and the earth. When

lightning occurs, two things happen. First there is a bright flash in the sky, then a deep rumbling noise is heard. The flash is the electricity. The noise, thunder, is caused by the rapid expansion of hot air around the lightning. Lightning can be dangerous. Never stand under a tree during a storm, because lightning tends to strike tall objects. To protect a building, a lightning rod is attached to the roof.

Rainbow—When the sun comes out after a storm, you can often see a rainbow. A rainbow is the reflection of the white light of the sun on the raindrops. As the light is reflected, it is divided into the colors red, orange, yellow, green, blue, indigo, and violet, which make up the white light. A rainbow will last only as long as there are droplets of water in the sky.

Today It Is Raining

Rain—When water droplets in clouds collect together they form bigger droplets. These bigger droplets collect together and make even bigger droplets which get too heavy to stay up so they fall to the earth as rain.

A storm is coming. Today is the day for a rain slicker and rain boots.

If It Rains Too Much—When there is too much rain, the rivers become very full and overflow their banks. The areas around the rivers then get flooded. Even a cloudburst, which is a very brief but violent storm, can cause flash flooding. This is because the soil cannot absorb the enormous amount of rainwater quickly enough.

If It Does Not Rain Enough—If there is not enough rain, the land gets dry and plants die. If the water shortage is not too bad farmers can get water by pumping it from under the ground. In wealthy countries there are many kinds of irrigation to help farmers.

Acid Rain—Sometimes polluted air is contained in the raindrops. That creates polluted raindrops. This polluted rain damages soil, plants, trees, and even buildings.

Where Rain Comes From—Very, very small drops of water evaporate from rivers, lakes, and oceans. These drops of water rise and form the clouds. Water even evaporates from the leaves of trees and plants. This is why the largest clouds form over forests and they get more rainfall.

Protecting Nature—The Amazon basin is a vast region in Brazil covered by dense tropical forests. These forests are needed to balance the earth's climate. Unfortunately these forests are being cut down. If all these trees are cut down there will be less rain in the world. People everywhere need to find ways to protect these important forests and the earth's other natural resources.

Solid Water

Ice Nuggets—Hail forms inside huge cumulonimbus storm clouds, mostly during summer. Because the highest and the lowest parts of the clouds have very different temperatures, violent rising winds can develop.

These rising air currents carry water vapor high into the air where it freezes and falls to the ground as hail. Hail is made up of layers of ice.
When hail falls, it can cause a lot of damage and ruin crops.

If you look at snowflakes under a magnifying glass, you will see how beautiful they are.

Snowflakes—In winter the water vapor inside the clouds can be transformed into thin slivers of ice that join together in the clouds. These are snowflakes—no two are the same. They look like flowers made of ice.

The Conquest of the Skies

Hot-air balloon

The Sky—Humans have always wanted to fly. Inspired by the flight of birds, through the centuries people have tried to construct wings like birds. Finally, airplanes and rockets were developed and used to discover the skies and outer space.

Hot-Air Balloon—The hot-air balloon rises because the balloon is filled with hot air, which is lighter than regular air.

The Wright Brothers airplane

The First Airplane—The first flying motorized machine was built by the Wright brothers. It made its first flight in 1903.

Blimps—Blimps are similar to hot-air balloons, but the important difference is that they have a motor and propeller.

The blimp "Norge" carried the explorers Amundsen and Nobile to the North Pole.

The Folcker E: German fighter plane used in World War I

Battles in the Sky—Aviation made great progress during World War I and World War II. All the countries involved in the wars wanted airplanes that could travel faster and higher.

The Spitfire: English fighter plane used in World War II

A6M Zero: Japanese fighter plane

Times of Peace—After the wars, airplane developers began to produce airplanes that could fly passengers and goods long distances. Jet propelled airplanes were developed and led the way to the development of rockets.

The De Haviland "Comet" was the first jet airplane to carry passengers in the 1950's.

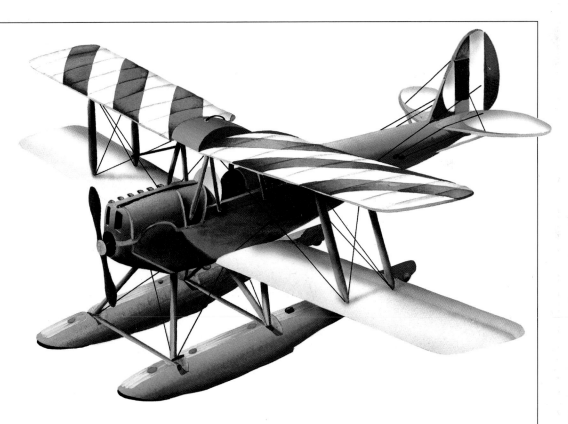

Hydroplanes are airplanes that can take off and land on water. Instead of wheels, they have floating landing gear. This is a Caproni CA 100, an Italian two-seater hydroplane used in the 1930's.

The Helicopter—This method of transportation was developed in the 1940s. Helicopters have become irreplaceable because they can remain stationary in the air and land in small areas.

The X15 was a rocket airplane. It set many records for height and speed.

Agusta Bell 206

The French Mirage IV: a modern bomber

The Fastest—The Concorde is the fastest passenger jet airplane in the world. It flies from New York to London in about 3 hours.

Concorde

From the Earth to the Moon— New methods of traveling through the air and through space are constantly being developed.

Around the Earth

Like a Ball—A globe of the earth is like a ball. It turns on its axis, which runs through the North and South Poles. The earth makes one full rotation every twenty-four hours. In this way every location on earth has sunlight for part of the time, and darkness for the rest.

Continually Turning—If the earth were to stop turning, one part of the earth would have constant sun and the other part would be in constant darkness. The plants and animals on the dark side would die because they need sunlight to survive. It would also be very cold. The snow would never melt and everything on that side of the earth would be covered with ice. Luckily there is no danger of that. The earth will continue to turn.

Reversed Seasons—While the earth is turning on its axis, it is also circling the sun. It takes one year to make a full journey. The seasons on earth change according to where the earth is on its trip around the sun. Because the earth is at an angle to the sun, when the northern hemisphere is close to the sun the southern hemisphere is farther away. So when it is summer in the north it is winter in the south. It seems strange, but in Australia you can have a picnic on the beach and go swimming on Christmas Day!

Shadows—The position of the sun on the horizon changes according to the seasons. In summer, the sun is high in the sky so shadows are shorter. In winter at the same time of day, the sun is lower in the sky so shadows are longer.

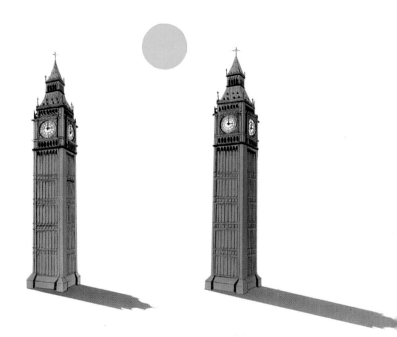

The shadow of this tower is shorter in summer than in winter at the same time of day.

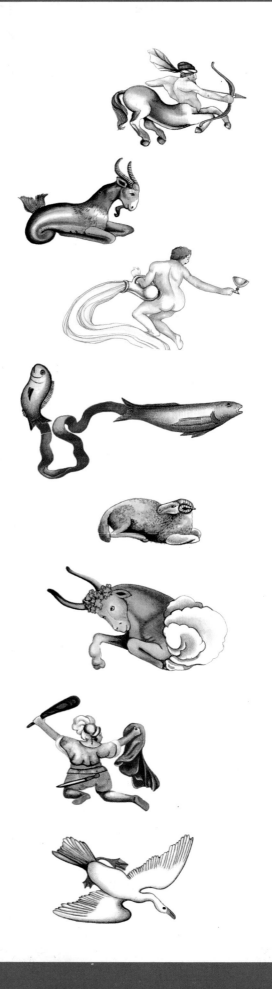

Sagittarius—Half-man and h
gallops through the skies with
bow and arrow.

Capricorn—He looks like a go
mermaid tail.

Aquarius—Rivers of stars from a
water pitcher flood the skies.

Pisces—These fish, tied together
swim peacefully across the skies.

Aries—This ram runs happily throug
the stars.

Taurus—The bull challenges the
hunter Orion.

Orion—A handsome hunter who was
killed by Scorpio, but he still travels
across the sky.

Cygnus—The swan flies over the
Milky Way.

Come See the

Constellations

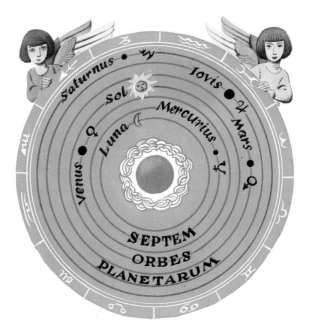

A fresco is a painting on a ceiling or wall. The
pictures on the following four pages were inspired by a
fresco in the Farnese Palace in Caprarola, Italy.

Gemini—Castor and Pollux are twin brothers.

Cancer—The crab has large claws.

Leo—The lion wants to be king of the sky as well as the forest.

Virgo—This beautiful young woman with wings is loved by all.

Libra—Libra can weigh all the stars on its scale.

Scorpio—Beware of the scorpion's poisonous tail.

Ursa Major—"Big Bear" is the easiest constellation to recognize. It contains the "Big Dipper."

Ursa Minor—"Little Bear" contains the "Little Dipper." Also among the stars in Ursa Minor is the very bright North Star—Polaris—by which sailors steer.

Very Big and Very Far Away

Is that girl holding a very small boy in her hands?
No, the boy only looks small because he is far away.
The stars also seem small, but that is because they
are so very far away. Some stars are as small as
the earth, and some are even bigger than the
sun. But because they are so far away they look
tiny enough to gather in your hands.

As Fast as Light

The Speed of Light— Scientists know that light takes time to move from one place to another. It travels at more than 186,000 miles per second. If a rocket could travel that fast, it would be able to travel seven times around the earth in just one second!

Sunlight—The light of the sun takes about eight minutes to reach the earth. This means that when we look at the sun, we see it as it was eight minutes earlier.

Many stars are so far away that their light takes millions of years to reach us. Some stars that we can see actually no longer exist.

A Very Long Trip—Some stars are so far away from us that it would take millions of years to reach them. The only way to travel to other solar systems is in our imaginations.

With your imagination anything is possible. Maybe if you wore magical seven league boots you might be able to travel faster than the speed of light.

The Moon

A Constant Companion—The moon revolves around the earth on its trip through space. Unlike the earth, which spins as it moves around the sun, the same side of the moon always faces the earth.

Phases of the Moon—The moon has no light of its own. The moonlight that we see is light reflected from the sun. From the earth we can easily see the moon. "There is a full moon!" we say, when we see the moon's illuminated sphere as a whole. But as the days pass we see less and less of the moon's round shape. At last it disappears completely. For a few days the night sky is dark, and then one night, a beautiful new sliver of moon appears. Each night it grows larger and larger until at last we see the moon as a glowing sphere again. This cycle takes 28 days.

Many Craters—If you look at the moon through a telescope you can see that it is full of craters.

Objects on the moon weigh about 6 times less than they do on earth.

These are huge indentations that have been made by meteorites—massive rocks hurling through space that crashed into the moon's surface a long time ago. There are some very high mountains, and vast plains on the moon that scientists call "seas." There is no rain or wind on the moon, so these seas do not have any water in them—just rocks and dust.

A Trip to the Moon—On July 21, 1969, Neil Armstrong, an American astronaut, walked on the moon. He was the first man ever to do it. The entire world saw it on television as it happened. To travel to the moon Neil Armstrong had to be specially equipped. Without his special spacesuit he could not have breathed. There is no air or water on the moon. There are only rocks, stones, and dust. Scientists plan to one day have a space station on the moon, but everything needed for humans to survive will have to be brought from the earth.

The air around the earth forms its atmosphere. The moon does not have an atmosphere. It is very hot on the side facing the sun and very cold on the other side. Astronauts have to wear spacesuits as protection from both the heat and the cold.

Mercury, Venus, Earth, and Mars

Mercury

Mercury—This is the second smallest planet in the solar system, and the one closest to the sun. It can be seen only just before dawn and just after sunset. People used to believe that it always turned the same side to the sun, but now we know that this is not true. Mercury rotates very slowly. The temperature on Mercury is so high that nothing could ever live there.

Legends—Many of the names of the stars and planets—like Cassiopeia and Orion, Mercury, Venus, Mars, and Uranus—are taken from the names of the Greek and Roman gods and heroes whom ancient Greeks believed lived on Mount Olympus, above the clouds in the sky.

Venus—This is the second closest planet to the sun. It is almost as big as Earth. Like Mars, the temperature on Venus is very high—about 900° F. The atmosphere around Venus is mostly carbon dioxide. In 1982 the Soviets landed two unmanned spaceships on Venus. They sent back lots of pictures of the planet. Just like the moon, Venus has many mountains and craters.

Venus

Earth—This is the third closest planet to the sun. It has a mild temperature and is the only planet with an atmosphere suitable for living things. It has one satellite, the moon.

Here are the nine planets that revolve around the sun: Mercury, Venus, Earth, Mars, Jupiter, Saturn, Uranus, Neptune, and Pluto.

Mars—This is the fourth planet from the sun. Astronomers once thought there might be life on Mars. But now they know that this is not so. In 1965 spaceships passed close to Mars for the first time and sent back photographs of the planet. No evidence of any form of life was found. Mars, like the moon and Venus, has craters formed by falling meteorites. Mars has two moons revolving around it: Deimos and Phobus.

Mars

Earth

Jupiter, Saturn, Uranus, Neptune, and Pluto

Jupiter—This is the largest planet in the solar system. It is fifth from the sun. It would take 1,300 planets the size of the earth to make one Jupiter. There are sixteen satellites revolving around Jupiter. It is surrounded by a very dense atmosphere that becomes liquid very close to the planet's surface.

Saturn—This is the strangest planet: it has rings that revolve around it as well as seventeen satellites. Saturn is just slightly smaller than Jupiter and very cold, because being the sixth planet from the sun, it is very far away. Its atmosphere is made up of gases that humans cannot breathe, so it would be impossible for us to live there.

Jupiter

This is Saturn: its rings are formed by a large quantity of dust and rocks suspended in space.

Uranus and Neptune—These planets are very similar. They are both larger than the earth. They are very far from the sun—seventh and eighth in the solar system. These two planets are very cold because the sun's rays are weak by the time they reach them.

Neptune

Uranus

Pluto—In our solar system this planet is the farthest (ninth) from the sun. It was discovered even before it was sighted! An astronomer noted that Neptune seemed to be attracted by an invisible planet. Fifteen years later another astronomer discovered that there was one more planet in the solar system. It was Pluto. He was able to photograph it. Pluto is not very large—it is about as big as the earth. Pluto and its satellite, Charon, are considered to be a double planet.

Pluto

The Sun

A Star— The sun is the star closest to the earth. It is made up of burning hot gases, so it is impossible to go near it. Any substance would burn immediately! Someday the sun will run out of gases to burn and will stop shining. But it is still a young star, so that will not happen for at least one billion years. If you look at the sun with a special telescope, you can see dark spots—these are sunspots. They are cooler places on the sun which burn less gas and look dark to us.

Like the Sun—Humans are often inspired by nature. Scientists are trying to produce energy the way the sun does. This is called nuclear fusion.

The sun has fascinated humans since ancient times. It has even been worshiped as a god. Artists have depicted the sun in many ways.

Nuclear fusion was used to create the hydrogen bomb. Now scientists are trying to create nuclear fusion in a more controlled way, so the energy can be used bit by bit—not all at once like a bomb. In this way people would be able to use the energy in their daily lives.

This is what the sun looks like through a telescope. You must always look at the sun through special filters, and never with the naked eye, because its rays are so strong they could blind you.

Observing the Sky

The Mysterious Sky—Since ancient times humans have been fascinated by the stars and planets. Some ancient peoples believed the sun, moon, and stars were gods and worshiped them. The Egyptians called the Sun "Ra" and the Moon "Iside." The Greeks called them "Helios" and "Selene"; the Romans called them "Phoebus" and "Diana." The Mayans offered human sacrifices to their sun god.

The Mayans did not have telescopes; they observed the sky through cylinders of jade.

The Telescope—In the 1600s a great Italian scientist named Galileo Galilei invented an instrument that allowed him to look at stars that were very far away and invisible to the naked eye. It was called a "telescope." Over time, telescopes became much larger and more powerful. Astronomers discovered that some celestial bodies produce radio waves as well as light. Today they use radio and optical telescopes to study the universe.

Beyond the Clouds—The earth's atmosphere is often hazy and prevents us from seeing the sky clearly. For this reason astronomers build their telescopes on top of mountains where the air is clearer. Manmade satellites are also used to study the stars. They carry special telescopes that transmit what they see to scientists on earth.

This is the giant telescope at Mauna Kea, Hawaii. It was completed in 1992. The mirror of this telescope is 32 feet in diameter.

The Night Sky

A Giant Umbrella—The stars in the sky seem to circle above our heads, like a giant umbrella. The only star that does not seem to move is the North Star. The stars in fact are still; it is the earth that is rotating—with us on it.

Planets—Not everything that shines in the night sky is a star. We can also see our own solar system.

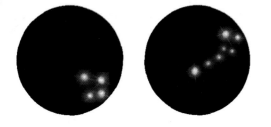

The night sky in the Northern Hemisphere is different from the night sky in the Southern Hemisphere. In America, which is in the Northern Hemisphere, the North Star is used for finding direction. In Australia, which is in the Southern Hemisphere, the Southern Cross is used. The North Star cannot be seen from there.

Our solar system is made up of the earth's moon and all the other planets. These heavenly bodies revolve around the sun. We can see them because they reflect the sun's light. The planets do not emit any light themselves.

Constellations—The ancient civilizations of Asia Minor, Assyria, Babylon, and Phoenicia believed it was very important to study the stars. They believed that events on earth and personal fortunes could be foretold by observing the sky. When they looked at the sky, they saw the stars in groups, or constellations. They named the constellations after what they seemed to look like—animals, people, or things.

The kangaroo lives in Australia, in the Southern Hemisphere. It can see the Southern Cross.

Stars in the Sky

Starlight—Stars vary widely in color, size, and brightness. They are blue, white, yellow, and red. Some are larger than the distance between the earth and the sun! Some are as small as the earth but very bright. That makes them seem much larger and nearer to the earth than they really are.

A barred spiral galaxy

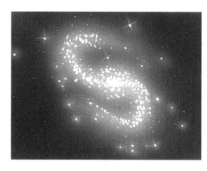

A White Stripe—If you look at the sky on a clear night, you can see a blurry white stripe. It is called the "Milky Way." It is made up of millions of stars, too far away to be seen individually.

When we stir a cup of hot chocolate with a spoon the bubbles form a spiral. The galaxies rotate in this way, taking millions of years to complete a single turn.

Together—Billions of stars often form groups called "galaxies." The Milky Way is our galaxy, which is a spiral shape. Since we are inside it, we cannot see the whole spiral. We can only see a part of our galaxy, where the stars are closest together.

An elliptical galaxy

A Greek myth says that Heracles stole a drop of milk from Hera. When the milk spilled it became the Milky Way.

A simple spiral galaxy

Galaxies—Galaxies can have different shapes; elliptical, barred spiral, or simple spiral. A simple spiral looks just like the spiral of bubbles that form in your cup of hot chocolate when you stir it.

Black Holes

Atoms—Everything that exists is made up of atoms. They are so small that no one has ever been able to see them. They never touch each other. There is always a space between one atom and the next. If all the atoms in the earth had no spaces between them, our planet would be only as big as a basketball.

Black Holes—When large stars die part of the star explodes into a cloud of gas. The rest becomes *compressed*—the atoms are pushed so close to each other that they almost touch. This matter, or "black hole," is so dense that other bodies are very strongly attracted to it. Any object that gets close to a black hole is drawn into it—even light, so it is invisible. How do scientists know that black holes exist? Because they can see stars being attracted to something invisible, and they guess this object is a black hole.

Big Bang—Many scientists believe that the universe was born 10 billion years ago in the explosion of an enormous mass. They call this explosion the "Big Bang." They think that this explosion created all the stars and planets that now exist. When scientists observe galaxies moving away from us, they believe this is still in reaction to the Big Bang.

A black hole is like a one-way funnel.
Once something enters its field of attraction,
it is sucked in—never to be seen again.

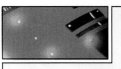

Extraterrestrials

UFO—This stands for "Unidentified Flying Object." This name is used for all objects that are seen in the sky and cannot be explained.

Life in Space—At one time it was thought that there might be life on Mars. People called the creatures that were believed to live there "Martians." They were described as little green people with antennas. Now we know positively there is no life on Mars.

Some people claim to have seen strangely shaped "flying saucers." There is no proof of their existence.

Do Extraterrestrials Exist?—Some people say they have met extraterrestrials, and claim to have gone aboard their spaceships. Scientists are positive that there are no other forms of life in our solar system. If some form of life has evolved in outer space, it is so distant that there is no way for us to make contact with it.

Noises—The universe is full of radio waves emitted by the stars. Scientists use radiotelescopes to listen to the sounds in space, and have an observation program that tries to distinguish among the strange "radio noises" in outer space. It is not easy. It is like trying to hear the sound of a bird chirping in a stadium during a sports event.

We Are Here

What is the Universe?—It is a portion of outer space that is occupied by stars, planets, and galaxies. To us the earth seems very large, but on a map of the universe our whole solar system would be smaller than a pencil dot.

Glossary

astronomer—someone who studies the universe beyond the earth's atmosphere.

atmosphere—the gases that surround the earth.

axis—an imaginary line that passes through the North and South poles, around which the earth rotates.

black hole—a large celestial body that has collapsed and become so dense that no light can escape from it.

celestial body—a large mass that exists in space such as a planet, moon, star, asteroid, or comet.

comet—a large mass of ice and rock that orbits the sun. As it nears the sun it develops a long bright tail pointing away from the sun.

constellation—a group of stars, as seen from Earth, that has been named after an animal or mythological figure.

crater—a large dent in the earth or a planet made by a meteorite, or by a volcanic eruption.

drought—a long period of no rain.

eclipse—when one celestial body temporarily passes in front of another. In a solar eclipse, the moon blocks out the sun. In a lunar eclipse, the earth's shadow covers the moon.

equator—an imaginary line around the middle of the earth, running from west to east.

evaporate—to turn into gas and disappear.

Fahrenheit—a scale for measuring temperature. Invented by a German scientist, Gabriel Fahrenheit (1686-1736). On the Fahrenheit scale the freezing point is 32°, and the boiling point is 212°. On the Celsius, or centigrade scale, the freezing point is 0°, and the boiling point is 100°.

galaxy—a system of stars and planets held together by gravity.

Galileo Galilei—an Italian astronomer (1564-1642) who invented the telescope and believed that the earth revolved around the sun, rather than the other way around.

gravity—the attractive force exerted by a celestial body.

hemisphere—half of the earth.

horizon—the boundary between the earth and the sky.

light year—5.87 million miles. The distance a ray of light travels in one year. Used to measure distances in space.

Mayans—an ancient tribe of Central American Indians, famous for their advanced astronomical knowledge and elaborate architecture.

meteor—small bodies of stone or metal that enter the earth's atmosphere and make a brilliant streak of light.

meteorite—a body from outer space that has passed through the earth's atmosphere and has come to rest on earth. They can be tiny or weigh up to 60 tons.

moon—a natural satellite that orbits a planet.

orbit—the path made by a celestial body as it revolves around another.

phases—the changes in the moon's appearance in the sky as the month progresses.

planet—one of nine celestial bodies that revolve around the sun.

pole—each end of the earth's axis: the North Pole and the South Pole.

pollution—fouling of the atmosphere, water, or land.

reflection—the return or bouncing of any rays such as light, heat, or sound off a surface.

satellite—a natural or manmade body that orbits a planet.

solar system—the sun, and the planets and moons that revolve around it.

trade winds—the nearly constant winds from the east that occur in the tropics and subtropics.

transmit—to send out, as in light or sound waves.

Tropic of Cancer—an imaginary line around the earth 23.5° north of the equator.

Tropic of Capricorn—an imaginary line around the earth 23.5° south of the equator.

Italian text and illustrations copyright © 1993 Dami Editore
English text copyright © 1994 Modern Publishing, a division of Unisystems, Inc.

Concept by Elisabetta Dami, Adrianna Sirena

U.S. edition designed by Barbara Lipp

U.S. text by Debby Slier

Illustrated by Cecilia Bozzoli, Alessandra Cimatoribus, Luana Frenno, Matteo Lupatelli,Claudia Melotti, Rosalba
Moriggia, Maddalena Motteran, Salvatore Palazzolo, Umberta Pezzoli, Maria Piatto, Mattia Pirro, Marina Vecchi

™World of Knowledge is a trademark of Modern Publishing, a division of Unisystems, Inc.
® Honey Bear Books is a trademark owned by Honey Bear Productions, Inc., and is
registered in the U.S. Patent and Trademark office.

Printed in EEC, Officine Grafiche De Agostini - Novara 1994
Bound by Legatoria del Verbano S.p.A.